Tao of Feng Shui

BOOK ONE

FUNDAMENTALS OF FENG SHUI

Tao of Feng Shui

BOOK ONE

FUNDAMENTALS OF FENG SHUI

SHAN-TUNG HSU, PH.D.

BLUE MOUNTAIN FENG SHUI INSTITUTE

specific purpose or activity. Feng Shui deals with how the environment affects us. The key to understanding its applications is to see it as the search for balance and harmony with nature.

But what is nature? It is something other than just the collection of natural objects – trees, water, rocks, birds, fish, and so on. Nature is whatever flows and exists, whatever energy manifests through. In ancient times, through lifelong observation and experience, people came to see how the sun rises and sets, the moon waxes and wanes, and dynasties rise and fall. They noticed certain patterns existing not only in nature but also in human life. These patterns are called "natural law" – but the Chinese idea of "law" here has a very specific quality. It does not mean law imposed from the outside, by a lawgiver. It means patterns emerging from the inner natures of things. The way that water moves on a surface, the way that veins form in marble, the way knots form on a tree trunk: these things have patterns that one can come to understand, that emerge spontaneously, without being forced or enforced. Ideally, the laws of human society are the same: they emerge out of the nature of human relationships, and are not handed down from on high. They are what we need to be fully human.

In the same way, to be fully human beings in the world, we need to acknowledge and move with the patterns that spontaneously emerge from who we are and what our world is. These patterns can be known, like the patterns of wind and water flow, from sympathetic observation and long familiarity. They are not simply vague "artistic" or "poetic" patterns – they can be described in fairly precise terms. It is the description of these patterns, and the terms that allow them to be discussed, that form the basis of the traditional Chinese sciences and cultural life. And it is the study of Feng Shui that can lead us into greater awareness of these patterns in all aspects of life.

This understanding, this wisdom, has actually existed for thousands of years in China. The highest goal of human life, in Taoist teaching, is to seek balance and harmony with nature. Taoist teachings stress that people should live, work, and sleep in accord with natural patterns. These teachings emphasize that one should eat from what is provided locally, according to the season, and should wake up with the sun and work, and rest after sunset. This is to be in tune with nature. By doing so, we are told, we should be able to live to the full extent of the human life span, up to a hundred twenty or so years.

Saving our planet, restoring the earth, living in harmony with nature, being at one with the universe – these slogans sound good, please our ears, and make us feel good. But they raise more fundamental questions: What is nature? What does it mean to be one with the universe? How does one be in harmony with nature? How do you restore the earth, and to what, since it is always changing anyway?

The chaos and confusion of human suffering is often brought on by human greed and ignorance. But many of the problems that have developed since the beginning of the industrial revolution really derive from the Western paradigm or model of the relationship between nature and humanity. With the Enlightenment, people in the West came to see themselves as being at the center of the universe, and came to regard nature as something that simply belonged to human beings. It became the common idea that man could conquer the world, and that nature was something to be shaped to fit human needs and desires. Because we own the land, we can make holes through mountains, build dams across rivers, or develop cities wherever we feel like it, even in a flood plain. We still call our planet Mother Earth, but we have decided to dominate and control our mother. For any species whose members have a life span of less than a century to think that they can own or control something with billions of years of history is, to say the least, an interesting notion.

As we have come to realize the sort of damage we have done, we have begun to think that we have, so to speak, been abusing our mother. We want to make up for this, and to restore her to what she was. But if we do this while still thinking that we are at the center of the universe, keeping to the old paradigm of the relationship between nature and humanity that led to the problem, we might make the same old mistakes, equally extreme but in the other direction. We want to do something for the Earth – but do we really know what the Earth wants? Does she really enjoy, or approve of, our new "positive" interference?

If the old paradigm is so problematic, what principles should guide us in repairing the damage we have done, and in restoring the planet? I believe we need to re-assess and re-examine our attitudes toward, and understanding of, nature. To establish a new paradigm for the human-nature relationship, we have to realize that human beings, like fish, frogs, or deer, are part of nature – not outside it or above it. We are at most transient passengers on our planet. We do not, and can not, own it.

What, then, does living in harmony with nature mean? To answer this question, let's examine how we live in harmony with people. To be friendly with someone, and live in harmony with them, we need to know their personality and temperament, their character, their strengths, and weaknesses. We have to be sensitive to their feelings and respect what they are. This is the first step toward developing a cordial relationship.

Most of us have a good enough understanding of how to get along with other people – but we don't do the same things when we are dealing with nature. When we go into someone else's house, we know enough to ask for permission – but do we ask for permission from the land? We build dams, highways, and cities to fit our purposes, but we hardly even imagine consulting with the land. We build cities in flood plains, or houses on steep slopes – and may have no problems for twenty or thirty years. But a single big flood will destroy the whole city. We call this a natural disaster – but nature never has disasters. Nature makes adjustments, in its process of continuing change, and we endure the results, some of which are the consequences of our actions.

When we want to build a house on property that we "own," what is the usual thing to do? We hire an architect, who makes plans, which are submitted to the relevant government agency for approval. If we did respect the land and nature, the first permission we asked would be from the land – permission to build a house of whatever size, to support a family of however many members. We would negotiate with the land – and the first "permit" we obtained would be from the land itself. Having obtained it, we would then bring the design – color, material, structure – and present it to the neighboring houses and trees, the rivers and rocks, and see if they could accept this structure as a neighbor. They might find it acceptable – or they might find the color and structures too eccentric, in which case we should adjust them accordingly. This, then, would be the second "permit." Only then would we be ready to apply for permission from governmental agencies.

This might seem like a radical, "New Age" idea. How can we ask for permission from land, rocks, or trees? But have you ever tried? This is, after all, not such a new idea. Traditionally, American Indians, before they set up their tents on a piece of land, pray for permission. Mongolian nomads, before settling down, will wait literally for days to obtain a sign of permission. They are more in tune with nature, and have more respect for nature. You might be surprised to find out how much information you can actually receive if you ask with a relaxed, humble, and open mind.

Why do we need to do this? Why should we be concerned about the Amazon rain forests or the depleted ozone layer? Isn't this all too far from anything that affects us in daily life – or anything we can have any control over? The reasons are twofold. The practical, realistic, and mundane reason is: for self-preservation. Just because the problems were first noticed by visionaries does not mean they are not real problems. It simply means that people with broader vision noticed them first. But there are other reasons that might not be so obvious – we might call them the spiritual reasons. Deep in our hearts, we are not only part of nature, part of the universe – we are an embodiment of the whole of nature, of the universe. Any damage, destruction, or imbalance that happens outside us also happens within us. Our spiritual life always calls for wholeness – and we respond to things that may seem remote, but which are actually also within us. According to holographic theory, an atom, a cell, a human body, a planet, the universe, are in a sense all the same, equally integral and whole. One might manifest on a larger scale, without being "more," or be infinitely small, without being "less".

It may seem that our need for survival is a legitimate excuse for such destruction. However, we can always survive with what is provided to us. Heaven is generous, and God never fails us. It is not necessary to ruin and destroy in order to survive. What really fuels the destruction is the bottomless reservoir of desire in the human ego. We have been provided everything we need – but instead of learning to recognize, receive, and accept what is provided to us, we ignore it, and go out to grab more, all due to a lack of sensitivity to know, see, and appreciate what is already here.

There is an inherent value and purpose in every part of this vast planet. A message is coded into each thing: a place to build a home, a place to cultivate, a place where water can flow, a place where natural things can remain undisturbed. This coding has an almost sacred quality: it carries the extra imperative that it is not to be violated. Yet the human-centered paradigm has totally ignored this.

A master sculptor doesn't impose a design on any random piece of rock. To create a specific design, a master sculptor may search for months to find the right piece – as though each rock has a spirit embedded in it, and the job of the artist is to bring it out. A piece of wood might look ordinary and nondescript, but a master artist might find a unique energy form within it. The artist's job is to release the energy, to help it manifest. What is true for a piece of rock or wood is also true for the larger land-scapes within which we live. Mountains, rivers, and plains have specific energy forms and spirits, specific patterns of energy flow. To understand these energy forms, the first thing one needs to do is to be in harmony with the land.

Everything nature provides us is there for a reason. Watermelons are available in the summer, to dissipate the heat of the summer. Nuts, harvested in the fall, provide us with the energy to get through the cold of winter. If there is a problem in a place, a solution to it should also exist there. A sickness peculiar to a locality should have a local remedy as well. But in modern life, it seems that we have come to increasingly disregard natural patterns. We eat, sleep, and work with almost no relationship to the cycles of the sun: sunset and sunrise are irrelevant because we have electricity. The four seasons don't matter because we have air conditioning. We can eat oranges or walnuts at any time of the year. We have taken over the design of the seasons – heat and cold, dark and light.

In Taoist teachings, there is also an understanding of land and space, in terms of form and energy. People can understand a good place to build a house or dig a well, how to coordinate structures with each other and with the entire landscape. This knowledge is called "Ti Li" (the law of the land) or "Kan Yi" (the law of Heaven and Earth). It provides guidance for establishing relationships with Heaven and Earth, that is, with nature. It has broad implications for all aspects of human life. Through history, however, this broad sense that this knowledge exists as a guide to life has been narrowed down to a more specific, limited application: guidance for building human dwellings. As such, it has become called Feng Shui, "Water and Wind." These terms, Water and Wind, represent the most fundamental forms of energy: permeating, nourishing, affecting all living things.

As the world surges into the next millennium, the rate of change keeps accelerating. Technological advances bring forth amenities at a faster rate, and at the same time life becomes too fast to have time to enjoy them. Wealth is increasing in the industrial countries, in drastic contrast with poorer countries. The pursuit of economic growth and the drive toward ever-increasing consumption are leading to global environmental problems – damage to the ozone layer, mineral-depleted farmlands, polluted rivers and water tables. International conferences, earth summits, and other expressions of concern show that there is not much consensus about what the true origins of the problems are – much less about what the solutions might be. The human race is facing one of its greatest challenges, but the challenge of this crisis may also bring forth a great opportunity.

Few people look to governments for any real solutions. Visionaries from all parts of the world, from every kind of background, have started grassroots movements promoting alternative directions for development. They have started farms emphasizing small-scale, multi-species models, as opposed to the large-scale monoculture style of industrial farming. They have created networks of self-sustaining cooperatives and co-housing arrangements, in place of big cities and large-scale housing projects. They recommend traditional herbal medicines, and healing techniques from all ethnic groups, with thousands of years of experience, instead of modern medicine, with its reported 100,000 or more deaths a year from side effects in the United States alone. But grassroots movements for alternative modes of life will need great effort and energy before they have a chance to take root or have any success in the struggle against big government and multi-national corporations. However, if enough seeds are planted around the world, and they are cultivated with enough energy, they will come to full blossom in time.

Many of these alternatives are promoted by romantic idealists responding to the crisis brought on by industrial development. However, we need to address this problem in a far more fundamental way, and not simply to revise certain surface phenomena. Otherwise, we may simply shift from one extreme to another.

Feng Shui provides the fundamental shift of orientation that can help us see a way out of the unproductive cycle of oppositions that contains and limits the usual attempts to solve these problems. This is the ultimate value of Feng Shui for people in the modern world: to enable us to come to terms with our world and its problems and go beyond them, without running away into a dream of an ideal past.

One Yin and one Yang

manifest Tao.

CHAPTER 2

Laws of Nature

The T'ai Chi symbol with its interlocked emblems of Yin and Yang, the Pa Kua (Ba Gua) mirror surrounded by the Eight Trigrams of the *I Ching* or *Book of Changes*, the sixty-four Hexagrams of that book, and the Five Elements – these are familiar to people with even a little contact with Chinese culture. They are the basic elements of a theoretical system that ties together all the traditional Chinese culture and sciences that have developed over the thousands of years of Chinese history. But a vital part of comprehending them is to not just study the theory, but to do what the Chinese did, to observe nature, and reflect on its patterns.

The understanding of the universe begins with observation. In ancient times, people observed the alternation of the day and night and the movement of the sky, the rotation of the seasons, the cycle of life and death of all living things, and the structures of human societies. Over long observation of the patterns of heaven, of earth, and of human society, they synthesized their observations into a more abstract and systematic understanding of the rhythms and patterns of the universe. From this, they developed a concept of the law of the universe, which they called the Tao or Way – the Way of the universe. This Way encompasses the fullness of the universe and every subordinate part of the universe. Human life and activity must inevitably be affected by the life and activity of the greater whole. Human beings, as a part of nature, are naturally subject to the same law. The Way for human beings should derive from the greater pattern: only thus can human beings achieve fullness of life.

According to the Taoist worldview, the finest substance of the universe is "ch'i," which might be called "vital energy." Ch'i is the basis of everything that has a form. Everything that exists is composed of ch'i and form, and the continuing interchange between ch'i and form is the basic process of the universe.

Since everything comes from ch'i, all things have a common base, which allows them to resonate together. Since everything resonates together, each thing is affected by every other thing, and changes in the greater universe naturally affect the lesser universe of the human body.

This concept of unity was expressed in one term, "T'ai Chi." The T'ai Chi is the embodiment of the Universe. The term literally means "the Great Extreme." It implies that everything in the universe is bound together, and nothing can escape the cycle of birth, growth, maturity, aging, and death. This concept refers not only to space but to time as well. It can mean the very beginning of everything, or the very end of everything, on any scale from the life of a gnat to the life of a universe. If there is birth, there must be death; if there is a beginning, there must be an end. Every thing in the universe is involved in an eternal cycle of birth and death, as long as it has an objective existence. Yet each thing also has its own cycle, no matter how big or small it may be – from a grain of sand or drop of water to a planet, a solar system, a galaxy, or beyond (even of something so big there is nothing larger, or so small there is nothing smaller). They all have their own patterns of development. They are also composed of many sub-levels, all of which in turn have their own cycles of birth and death. Every entity is a T'ai Chi, and every cycle is a T'ai Chi. Every thing is complete, is a whole, has its own cycle, and is connected to other things.

Much of this can be found in the now universally familiar T'ai Chi symbol – a circle composed of two fish-like parts, colored black and white, with a white dot within the dark area, and a black dot within the white area.

Diagram 2.1   *T'ai Chi*

Let's consider the meaning of this diagram. The circular outer form means that a universe always exists as a circular form, in both space and time. The planets, the sun, moon, and stars, and even the atoms, have circular forms. The cycles of time – day and night, life and death – also have a circular form. In other words, they are not linear: there is no definite beginning or ending, but in fact every beginning is an ending. Every point is both a beginning and an ending. This has many implications for understanding how things work, and how human beings should conduct themselves.

YIN-YANG PRINCIPAL

The two aspects, the dark and light aspects, represent the two polarized forces (known as Yin and Yang) or aspects within every T'ai Chi – within every thing, every process, every action, every thought. Their relationship is dynamic, not static; intermingled, not pure or isolated; interacting, not disconnected. The white dot in the dark side and the dark dot in the white side represent the Yang within Yin and the Yin within Yang – because the dot is a circle, it too is a complete T'ai Chi. Each contains the seeds of the other; without this, they would not be able to transform into each other.

The relationship between Yin and Yang is traditionally described as having four aspects: Yin and Yang unify and oppose; Yin and Yang entail each other; Yin and Yang increase and decrease; Yin and Yang transform into each other.

Yin and Yang Unify and Oppose

In the universe, every phenomenon consists of two aspects – up and down, left and right, heaven and earth, dynamic and static, hot and cold; the ultimate contrast is that between ch'i and form. These two aspects are separate, but unify into one phenomenon or dimension of experience. Because they are separate, they create a momentum for things to develop; because they are unified, they maintain a dynamic balance and integration. Things develop and decline through the mutual constraint and cooperation of Yin and Yang. This is the origin of the cycle of birth, growth, decay, and death. All cycles of human life, physiological to psychological, are rooted in Yin-Yang transformation and interaction.

YIN & YANG

Earth · Heaven

Moon · Sun

Night · Day

Mother · Father

Female · Male

Down · Up

Right · Left

Cold · Hot

Water · Fire

Mountain · Water

Static · Dynamic

Inhale · Exhale

Close · Open

Horizontal · Vertical

Retreat · Advance

Failure · Success

Matter · Function

Form · Chi

Square · Circular

Interior · Exterior

Soft · Hard

Table 2.1   *Yin-Yang Table*

Yin and Yang Entail Each Other

No aspect of the one can exist without the other: if there is no up, there can be no down; if there is no left, there can be no right; if there is no birth, there cannot be death. One aspect can exist only if the other exists as well. In the world of nature, the fundamental polarity is that between ch'i and form. If a living body has no ch'i, it cannot have form, and vice versa: without form, the function cannot manifest, and without ch'i, there is no physiological transformation, and thus no life. If there is Yin without Yang ("solo yin"), or Yang without Yin ("solo Yang), there can be no growth or transformation. Yin in isolation cannot give birth; Yang in isolation cannot grow.

Yin and Yang Increase and Decrease

Yin and Yang are in contrast and also interdependent, but they never exist in a static position or state. They are always changing. If one is deficient, the other is excessive; if one is increasing, the other is decreasing. In normal situations, the increase and decrease will have a certain limit, and it is this limit that allows them to maintain a dynamic balance. If they exceed that limit, the situation is no longer normal. On the individual level, this produces sickness; on the social level, this produces social chaos.

Yin and Yang Transform Into Each Other

In normal circumstances, Yin and Yang also change back and forth. Day changes to night, and night changes to day. Things can transform into each other because each contains the seed or possibility of the other. Therefore, any success bears the seed of failure, and any failure bears the seed of success and rebirth. In extreme cases, a quantitative change can become a qualitative change: when a ball is launched upward, its course is Yang; when it reaches the limit of its movement, it begins to fall, and its course becomes Yin.

All of these patterns can be seen at every level of the universe, every walk of life, all stages of human affairs. In Taoism, the highest human achievement is attaining the Tao. But what is Tao? The Tao is the basic law of nature. A classical saying is that one Yin and one Yang constitute the Tao. It is the equilibrium of Yin and Yang that lead to the Tao. When you take your body as a T'ai Chi, it implies that there should be a balance between your physical body and your spiritual body.

Yin and Yang are not things; they are attributes of things. Heaven is Yang and Earth is Yin, but Yang is not Heaven, nor is Yin Earth. When we consider human beings as a group, they can be seen as either male or female, and in that context male is Yang and female is Yin – but again, Yang is not male, nor is Yin female. When we say that the highest human virtue is understanding the Tao and living accordingly, that means living in a condition in which Yin and Yang are in equilibrium, not just in the body, but at all levels of existence.

Since the T'ai Chi also refers to multiple levels of organization, and all the levels are connected, when we talk about imbalance it is not simply a matter of balance within our own system, but also of balance within the greater system of which we are a part. We must be in balance within ourselves, body and soul; as individuals, we must be in balance with society. As a society, we should be in balance with nature, and so on.

People talk about "harmony with nature." To be in harmony means to be in balance. When things are in balance, they resonate. When they resonate, all the ch'i is connected; when ch'i is connected, it flows. This is why it is important to see beyond form to the presence of the ch'i. If anything goes wrong, we trace the problem

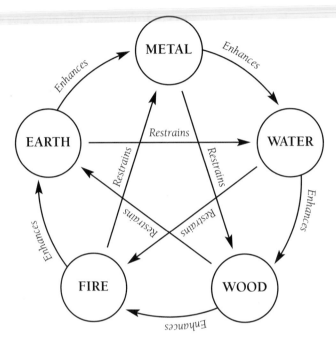

Diagram 2.2   *Five Element Relationship*

Just as Yin and Yang are closely connected with each other, affect each other, enhance each other, and control each other, these Five Elements are closely connected with each other and affect each other. Each one can enhance or be enhanced, restrain or be restrained. The diagram above shows the relationships: the outer circle shows the relationship of enhancement; the inner star shows the relationship of restraint or control.

Every life cycle can also be seen to fall into five phases. Things that are in the same phase resonate with each other. Thus, East relates to Spring; Spring relates to Green; Green relates to Birth. Winter, on the other hand, is associated with dark and cold. This concept has been applied with great sophistication in Chinese medicine. It can be seen from the table that the internal organs each belong to one of the five groups. Thus a heart problem (Fire) could be associated with Wood (liver),

Earth (spleen), Water (kidney) or Metal (lung). A doctor must always see the whole system to find the source of the problem, and make necessary adjustments. This is called a "holistic" approach, because it is based on the whole organism.

What is true for the human body is also true for society. Social problems cannot be solved in isolation. Everything affects everything, in various degrees. The basis of Chinese thinking is that human beings are part of the whole universe. The human cosmos should follow the law of the bigger cosmos.

Yin and Yang and Five Element Theory are regarded as the basic laws of the cosmos. Thus all Chinese traditional culture and sciences are derived from an understanding of these two systems. Medicine, literature, government, warfare, astronomy – all look to these concepts for inspiration and knowledge, and apply them accordingly. To fully understand Yin and Yang and the Five Elements is to fully understand the Tao, to fully understand universal truth. This is the foundation on which the whole science and art of Feng Shui is built.

When human beings build a dwelling – a cottage, a village, or a city – they have to look to the balance of Yin and Yang within, and coordinate all the associated aspects of the Five Elements. The better the association, the more harmonious the dwelling will be; the more balanced Yin and Yang, the more beneficial the dwelling will be for those who live there.

In later chapters, we will discuss the practical application of these concepts for site selection, building design, and other specific issues.

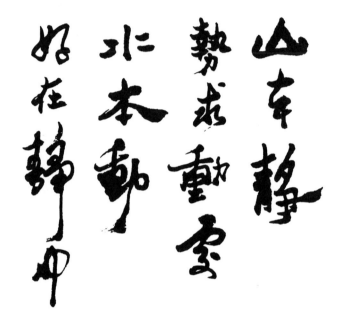

山本靜
勢求動雲
水本動
好在靜中

The innate nature of the mountain is static (yin).

Therefore, good mountain has a dynamic quality.

The innate nature of the water is dynamic (yang).

Therefore, good water has a tranquil quality.

CHAPTER 3

The Big Picture:
Structure On The Grand Scale

As we mentioned in the last chapter, everything in the universe, from an atom to a galaxy, is a T'ai Chi – is a whole cosmos in itself. It is composed of Yin and Yang, and Yin and Yang continually change, transform, and strive for balance.

With this in mind, we can look at the large-scale landscape of our planet, and examine it to see how it is in fact a universe of its own, a complete T'ai Chi. In general, in applying Feng Shui concepts to our planet, we can first distinguish between land masses and bodies of water; and then from the overall land masses we can also distinguish higher mountains, lower hills, and flat ground. Looking to the extremes for the Yin and Yang polarity, we can say that the high mountains represent one aspect, and the water the other. Within the Feng Shui context, which looks at energy flow in an environment, the mountains, with their static stability, would represent the Yin quality, while water, with its dynamic changeability, would represent the Yang quality.

Good or balanced energy derives from the quality of balance or harmony of a particular configuration of Yin and Yang. The flat ground between water and mountains is the spot toward which human beings naturally gravitate when developing a village, city, or metropolis. Where the water (Yang) and mountains (Yin) meet, that is where the place of balance is, the energy spot. Smaller hills, between the flat ground and large mountain, often define a space in which energy can collect, and by providing boundaries, provide protection for the spot to prevent the energy from being dispersed.

Mountains, small hills, flat ground, and water: these four features fully describe a landscape. Their properties manifest the character, quality, and quantity of the energy of the land. To understand the land is to understand these four features – not only their quality, quantity, and scale, but also the coordination of the features and their intensities.

It is easy to understand scale as a matter of the proportion or size of the features, but quality is not so obvious. What makes some features better than others? What makes some mountains better than other mountains, for example? The key is to look for the nature of the balance of Yin and Yang that compose the feature. Just as warmth is desirable in the winter, but not in summer, so a mountain, inherently Yin, needs some Yang features to bring the Yin qualities into balance. Thus a mountain with such Yang traits as a lively form, lush vegetation, and abundant animal and bird life will be an especially well-balanced mountain. A rocky, rigid mountain with little plant or animal life is too much Yin, and not as enlivened by an interaction with Yang; such a mountain is thus less desirable. People often refer to a mountain as a "dragon," and a good mountain will resemble a lively "dragon," and not a dead, depressed, or lazy one. (This does not mean that this only applies to mountains that look like the conventional image of a dragon – any similarity to an animal form is relevant in assessing the energetic qualities of a mountain. The full details of these patterns will be covered in our forthcoming book on applications of Feng Shui in exterior environment.)

The same considerations apply to water. To be good, the Yang qualities inherent in water will require Yin traits to achieve a fruitful balance. But such a thing as a tranquil and peaceful body of water (a lake or calm river, or a protected inlet of the sea) is closer to ideal. A raging river, a thundering waterfall, or an unmoderated ocean, which embody an intensification of Yang with more Yang, and not much internal balance, are less ideal. The Feng Shui classics say that where rivers are swift and raging, the people and land are generally poor, and that where the rivers slow and become peaceful, the people and land become richer.

The size of the flat ground is proportional to the amount of energy it can hold, which in turn connects with the potential growth of settlements. The larger the flat ground, the larger the energy spot, and the larger a city built there can and will become.

Small hills adjacent to the flat ground (the energy spot) not only define or delimit the energy spot, but also provide protection for it. This is why these are called Guardian Hills. Again, the quality and quantity of these small hills also affect the quality, quantity, and intensity of the energy spot. These factors are assessed much as they are for mountains, but since the hills also function as transformers, bringing the energy down to usable levels for the sake of the settlement, they should be understood as functioning at a milder level.

Mountains, being static and stable, provide the force for stability, the force of support. The guardian hills provide protection for the flat ground, where the energy collects. The flat ground is the energy spot, the nourishing space in which activities can occur. Water, flowing through the lowest places, confines and shapes the energy flow; it also provides an open field of vision which allows for expansion. When these features are good, and are well balanced, the Feng Shui of the landscape is good.

These are the features that constitute the Feng Shui model of the structure of any T'ai Chi, any universe, no matter what the scale, from largest to smallest. These four qualities are also the qualities required for any successful activity. In fact, since they constitute a truly universal model, based in an understanding of the Yin-Yang interaction, they can be applied to any aspect of life, individual or social.

The mountain feature, as a source of energy, support, and stability, is also the source of control. It becomes a metaphor for power, political or military. A country with great political or military influence usually has a strong mountain configuration.

Water features represent flow and traffic, and are thus metaphors for trade, commerce, and money. Economically successful countries have access to good, large bodies of water. Most large business centers are on rivers, oceans, or lakes.

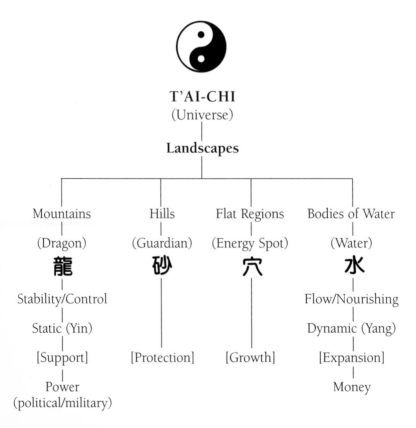

Diagram 3.1   *The Four Features and Their Metaphors*

Landscape not only affects political and economic issues: it also shapes the character and personality of the people who reside in it. People who live in cities on low ground, near water, will be very different from people living in high mountains. Even among cities near water, the quality and position of the guardian hills will affect the natures and personalities of the people who live in the cities. Buddhists say we are what we think; nutritionists, that we are what we eat; but it is even more valid to say that we are what we live in, both on a large scale and on smaller scales.

If we have a good understanding of the landscape of a country or a place, we will have a pretty good idea about the people, and the society, that occupy that country or that place. The energy manifesting through the landscape also manifests through the society and culture of the people who live there. Take, for example, the United States, bordered by the Atlantic in the east and the Pacific in the west, the two greatest bodies of water on the planet. The United States, in being defined by these bodies of water, can be said to be defined by money; indeed, economic issues are often the defining issues for this country and its people. With the two great oceans, the five Great Lakes, the great rivers within it, and the Gulf of Mexico to the south, it is no surprise that the United States possesses wealth and abundance. The two great mountain ranges, in the east and west, run parallel north and south: they shape the country, and hold it together. They provide strong political power. The vast open spaces between them and beyond them provide more room for free spirits and open minds, generosity and creativity, the basic traits of the American people. On the other hand, along with this often comes naiveté.

Japan, composed of four big islands surrounded by abundant water, also manifests great economic power. But Japan's flat land is limited, squeezed between water and mountains, and allows little space to maneuver. This lack of the flat space that would constitute a buffer zone makes the people who live in Japan feel less secure, and more inclined to protectiveness and defensiveness. For decades, Americans have wondered why it is so difficult to penetrate the Japanese market, and why the Japanese protect it so rigidly. This protectiveness derives from the nature of the landscape and the defensiveness it mandates.

Most Japanese mountain ranges, being smooth and connected, provide a cohesive force that binds Japanese people into a well-integrated whole. The clear image of Mount Fuji, the symbol of Japan, provides Japanese with a strong national identity. As the flat land is constricted between the mountains and the water, there is little space between the shift from one extreme to the other: this sharp polarization also manifests in Japanese character, in which appear, in vivid contrast, beauty and ugliness, violence and peacefulness.

For China, the Himalayas are the source of energy and power: all other mountain ranges radiate from there, as do the rivers that flow into the Pacific and the South China Sea. Great mountains and great rivers provide excellent Feng Shui features for China, and have nourished a great culture. In contrast to the United States, where the mountain ranges are parallel, the mountain ranges in China radiate outward, dispersing and scattering their power rather than containing it. They are not closely connected. The founding father of modern China, Dr. Sun Yat-sen, once lamented that Chinese were like a pan of sand, unable to stick together. This is a reflection of the basic configuration of the land. At the same time, tens of millions of Chinese have spread all over the world, and even after many generations they still identify themselves as Chinese. They identify with Chinese culture, because they feel connected to the same source, just as the Chinese mountains all trace back to the Himalayas.

In applying the features in this metaphorical way, it is important to continue to look at the balance of qualities within them. The Philippines, for example, have abundant water surrounding a thousand islands, but this does not correlate with economic strength, because the Yang side is over-strong in the absence of a strong Yin quality. In other words, there is no clear, defining mountain structure. Lack of a good leading mountain structure means a lack of powerful leadership and stable government, and as a result, the imbalance does not manifest in the form of balanced energy.

Although water is a metaphor for money, it is important to remember that it is not equivalent to money. Many people who have studied a little Feng Shui take the metaphor too literally, and think that just putting a fountain in a courtyard or in the living room will make you rich. If this were true, poor boat people in Asia should be very rich, because they live surrounded by water.

Beyond features as such, there is also the issue of form. The whole landscape is a form, and form defines energy just as energy manifests through and as form. In the case of India, with a great mountain to the north, and surrounded by the Indian Ocean, these powerful features have nourished a great culture with great traditions. But it does not have its fair share of economic and political strength, largely because of the particular form of the subcontinent, as we will explain in a later chapter.

We have talked about the quality and quantity of the four features. Their interaction and coordination is just as important. A piece of flat ground between two mountains will have a different energy than a similar piece of ground between two bodies of water, or with mountain on one side and water on the other.

What is the best kind of coordinated composition of these features – what model provides the ideal integration of the features? In our first chapter we said that human beings should take nature as a model: for human dwellings, the best natural model is the human body.

In their most general aspect, the four features have the following functions: mountains support, hills protect, the energy spot nourishes growth, and water allows expansion and receives and shapes energy. In the human body, the support comes from the spine, at the back of the body. Arms, legs, and ribs, providing protection, are on the sides. The important organs and functions are in the center. And the openings that allow for interaction with the world – eyes, nose, and mouth especially – are in front. This is why the classical Chinese Feng Shui model for a city prescribes that there be a mountain behind, water in front, and hills on both sides.

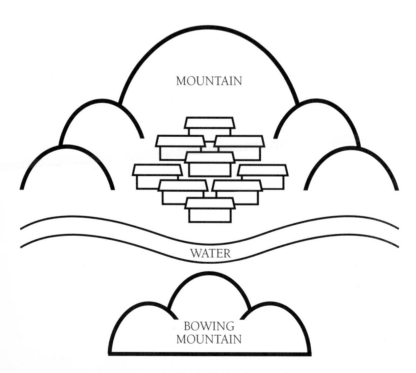

Diagram 3.2   *Classical Model of a Village Site*

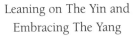

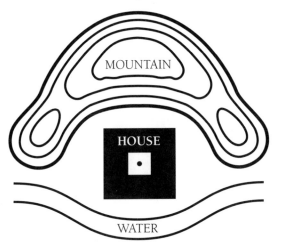

Encircled by Golden Belt

Diagram 3.3 *Classical Model of a House Site*

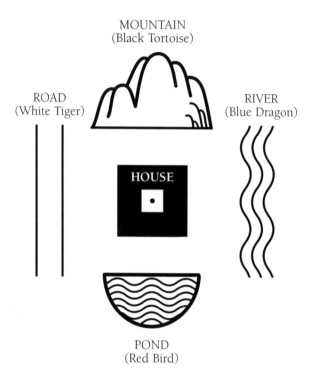

MOUNTAIN
(Black Tortoise)

ROAD
(White Tiger)

RIVER
(Blue Dragon)

HOUSE

POND
(Red Bird)

Diagram 3.4 *Classical Model of a House Site*

In addition to these four features, there is another important feature, which is orientation. Orientation, however, is usually predetermined by the existing positions of the mountain and water: if the mountain is to the north and the water is to the south, the orientation will naturally be toward the south. It is not possible to take orientation in isolation; it only makes sense when taken in combination with the other features. Most of the classical Feng Shui texts take the four landscape features as constituting the core of Feng Shui knowledge, no matter what scale or application they may take as a focus. However, over the centuries, as Feng Shui became influenced by astrology, people started to emphasize orientation, and many "cosmological" schools developed that emphasize orientation above, and even independent of, the other features. These are the schools that emphasize the use of the Feng Shui compass. There are many controversies among these different schools, and we will deal with the cosmological approach in a later book in this series.

When we begin, we need to understand the function of the features. The next step is to grasp how they are coordinated into a general model that resonates with the structure of the human body. Only then is it possible to begin to understand how these features can be used to analyze any unified entity – that is, any T'ai Chi – at any scale: a planet, a country, a city, a house, or a room.

Ideal Feng Shui:

the dragon is real,

the energy spot is precise,

the guardians are present,

and water embraces

CHAPTER 4

The Fundamental Feng Shui Model

"To see the world in a grain of sand, and to see Heaven in a flower" – Blake's saying reflects the "holographic" concept of the universe. A grain of sand and the universe are both complete T'ai Chis; flowers and Heaven both manifest truth and beauty, but on a different scale.

In practice, this means that everything we see on one scale can be translated to a smaller scale (or a larger one). In the previous chapter, we discussed a Feng Shui model from a large landscape point of view. This model involved the Mountain, the Hills, the Energy Spot, and the Water: metaphors for support, protection, growth, and expansion. Using the principle of translation from one scale to another, we can map this same model onto a small village, a house, or even a single room.

In an ideal small village, there will be some kind of supporting mountain, contoured protecting hills, a body of water, and a site that nestles within these features (see diagram 3.2). For a house, the building or land behind the house correspond to the "mountain," the houses on either side represent the "guardian hills," the street or open space in front corresponds to the "water," and the house itself will naturally occupy the energy spot. These four features are essential prerequisites for a good Feng Shui site.

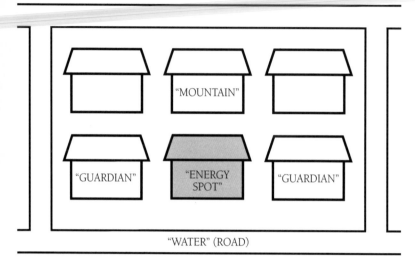

"WATER" (ROAD)

Diagram 4.1   *Ideal House Model*

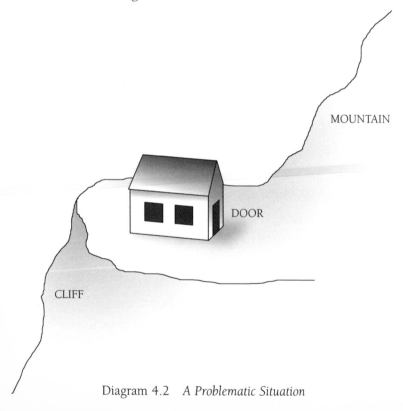

Diagram 4.2   *A Problematic Situation*

On the other hand, if there is a cliff or ravine behind the house, or if the front door faces a big hill or huge building, or the house is isolated and without neighbors, or the house stands on a steep slope, with no flat ground, then one or more of the four features is defective. Some essential element of a good house is missing.

Let's look first at a smaller and more manageable scale – say a small office. The wall behind the desk where one sits is the mountain feature. The two walls on the left and right are the guardian hills. The door and the open space toward the front are the water features. The chair and desk, then, are the energy spot. Thus, even in a small office, the four fundamental features of a Feng Shui site are present.

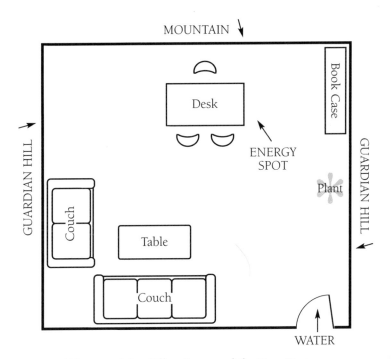

Diagram 4.3   *Office Space and the Four Features*

In the ideal Feng Shui model, the support should be behind you. Naturally, if you sit against a wall, you feel much more secure, and you naturally relax. If you sit facing a wall, with an open space or a door behind you, you cannot be as relaxed, and there will be less available energy. This kind of psychological and physiological response is universal. It has nothing to do with Asian theories or Oriental paradigms. Nowadays, however, people rely more and more on logic and reason, or worse, do things habitually or mechanically, rather than connecting to their inner feelings. This is why one so often sees the desk pushed up against a window, and the door behind the person at the desk. With this kind of configuration, it is likely that the desk will not be used very often, or that time spent there will not be very productive. Chances are, it will be used to write a few checks or an occasional note; it will not be used for serious work.

When there is no support behind you, as in this case, naturally there is a feeling of insecurity. The human brain, with its history of meeting evolutionary challenges, automatically puts aside a certain amount of energy for protection – so the energy left for other uses will be less than a full charge.

Furthermore, with the window in front, as soon as you raise your head, your eyes look out, and your energy goes outward with your vision. The mind will tend to wander and be unfocused, rather than concentrated. It will be hard to be productive at such a desk.

There is an ancient Feng Shui saying: "Something to lean on at the back; embracing arms on both sides; a spacious opening in front: this is already a good Feng Shui structure. If you truly understand this, you already have a full grasp of Feng Shui." In fact, Feng Shui principles are really simple – but it is not easy to grasp and apply these simple concepts, perhaps just because they are so simple.

This concept is a very powerful tool, and an intensely practical working model in any attempt to understand and work with Feng Shui at any scale, large or small – city, house, room, or even a painting or other design. Rather than trying to remember hundreds of rigid Feng Shui rules – rules that often will not be adequate to a particular concrete situation, or sometimes be misleading or even false – one can simply rely on this four-featured model as the primary tool for design and analysis.

Let's look at the simple task of where to put the bed in a bedroom. In diagram 4.4, there are four ways of placing a bed (A through D). Which one is closest to being ideal? Let's examine them one by one, using the four features.

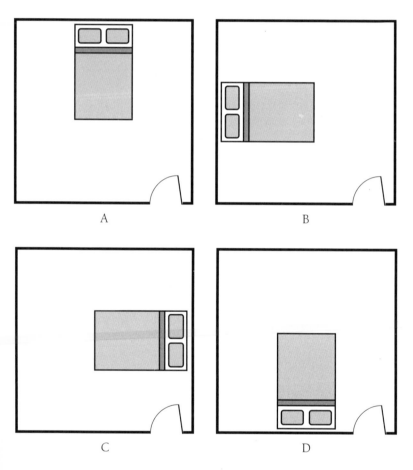

Diagram 4.4   *Bed Placement (Without Window)*

The Mountain

Rooms A, B, and C have a solid wall (the mountain, the most important feature) behind the head of the bed. In room D, the door is on the right side of the wall behind the bed, so the support is not as complete.

The Guardian Hills

Rooms A, B, and D have walls on both sides of the length of the bed, so the guardian hills are present. In room C, there is a door on the left, so one of the guardians is missing.

The Energy Spot

In this situation, the energy spot is the location of the bed, and the examples are all equal.

The Water

The entrance is regarded as the source of water. According to the model, water should be in front. In rooms A and B, the entrance is diagonally in front: this is ideal. In C, water is to one side, and in D, water is at the back: neither are good.

The four features of A and B follow the ideal set out by the model; C and D have flaws – either missing guardian or weak mountain, or water in the wrong direction.

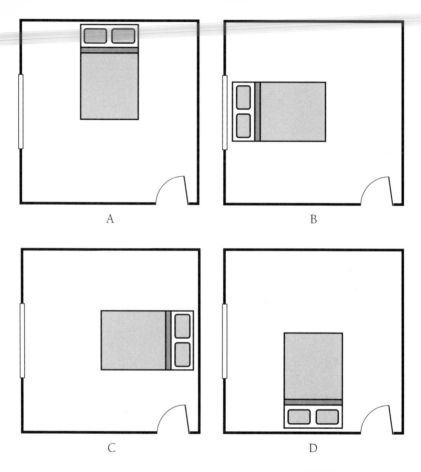

Diagram 4.5   *Bed Placement (With One Window)*

What happens if we put a window on one wall of the bedroom, as shown in diagram 4.5? Now, in room B, there is a window behind the bed. The support, the most crucial feature, is missing. This makes it worse than any of the others, and A is now the only ideal arrangement.

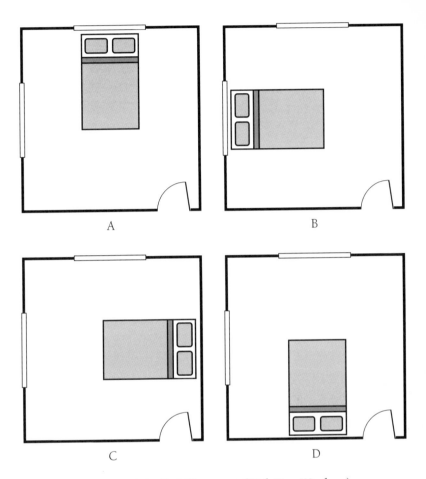

Diagram 4.6 *Bed Placement (With Two Windows)*

Nowadays, because people value light and view, some builders try to make sure that every room has both. It often happens, as in diagram 4.6, that a bedroom will have windows on two walls. In this case, both A and B are without support in back. In such a situation, it is impossible to put a bed in an ideal location. This over-emphasis on light and view in a bedroom is a mistake, since a bedroom is supposed to be a quiet and restful (Yin) room, and not a location of outward-reaching activity.

But why should we wish to arrange a bedroom according to the ideals of the Feng Shui model? Why is it necessary to have the water in front and the mountain behind? What's wrong with having a window in back, or a door behind?

As we said in the previous chapter, the ideal is to follow the natural model: nature presents the model by which things are best nourished and nurtured. This is exemplified through the human body. If we follow the natural model, the results will be good; the more one deviates from the ideal model, the more negative the results will be. For example, a window behind the bed can lead to an increased tendency to get sick, to have insomnia, or, for a couple, a tendency for the relationship to be empty. A door in back or to one side also implies poorer sleep or a tendency to get sick. This is not a matter of belief: it has been observed and validated throughout history.

This Feng Shui model can apply to any room or situation, just as it does in an office or bedroom. But each room also has its own function, and so the application of the model requires certain adjustments.

In real life, however, we are often given situations within which there are limitations. It is not always possible to find an ideal situation, so we are often left with trying to apply Feng Shui concepts to try to improve things as far as they can be, or at least to reduce the amount of damage.

For example, in diagram 4.7, there is a window on the north side; on the west side there is a closet with bathroom. The only place left for the bed is on the south side, which is missing part of the mountain, and also has water coming from behind. What can we do?

One popular approach in the United States is to put a mirror directly across from the door, as in diagram 4.8. The idea is that if people come from behind while one is in bed, one will be able to see them – if one is looking at the mirror at the time. This solution is imaginative, but it is basically merely psychological. The need to keep watching the mirror is itself a burden; one will still be unable to relax or let go completely.

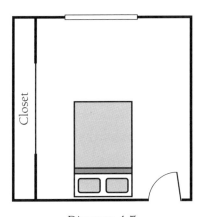

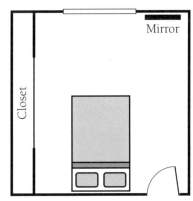

Diagram 4.7
Not Ideal Bed Placement

Diagram 4.8
Not Ideal Remedy

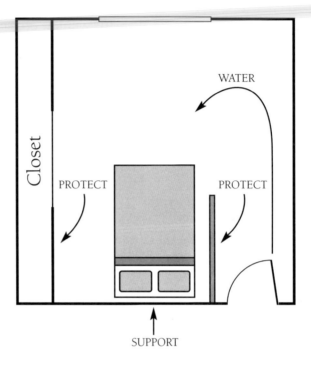

Diagram 4.9   *Ideal Remedy for Bedroom With Closet and Window*

This kind of approach ignores the fundamental and most basic concepts of Feng Shui. A correct approach is always grounded in the application of the four features. An ideal solution is shown in diagram 4.9. A partition is added next to the bed, near the entrance. With this partition, the mountain is complete. Both guardians are present, and the water now comes from the front.

Every remedy, then, should be derived from an analysis based on the application of the four features, and not from faith in mysterious gadgets, or in rationalizations derived from psychological guesswork.

In our daily life, we are always finding that we gravitate toward favorite spots – at home, or in a restaurant, for example – and avoid certain others. We do this intuitively, often without knowing why. Once we understand the four features and their effects, these habits and intuitions very quickly start to make sense. Feng Shui is neither mysterious nor complicated. It is not mysterious because it fits well with common sense. It is not complicated because, once one understands the fundamental principles, one is able to grasp much of the subject.

Just by grasping the model of the four features, it is possible to see why one store might be very successful – or why another might continue to be unsuccessful no matter how many management teams have done their best.

From the human point of view, the universe has three components: Heaven, People, and Earth. Of these, Heaven represents time, and Earth represents space. Feng Shui mostly focuses on factors of space. When space – one third of the equation – is defective, the human part of the equation has to be especially strong to achieve success.

To understand this concept is one thing; to use it skillfully is something else. One of the keys to successful application of the concept is understanding the matter of relative scale. When we talk about the four features, they should be put in perspective. For example, if there is a big lake or even an ocean ten miles in front of your house, or a mountain ten miles behind it, these features do not really apply to your house. The actual water feature for a house would be a street (or small stream or pond) near the house. Similarly, the mountain for the house would not be some geographic feature many miles away, but the structures or land features to the back of the house. Again, though the guardians to a house are the houses on either side, those houses are not guardians to a room in the house. For a room, the guardians are the walls on either side. In making any analysis, scale must be correctly understood, so that the relevant features can be identified and assessed.

These four features are powerful analytic tools – but the most fundamental consideration in assessing the impact of these features is the balance of yin and yang. Those supporting and being supported, and those protecting and being protected, have to be in an appropriate scale to be in balance, to reach harmony.

If a small building is located right at the foot of a sharply rising mountain, the mountain becomes no longer an ideal support, but an overpowering, dominating influence. This is far from ideal, because of the imbalance involved. In the same way, if a company needs financial support from an investor, the best investor is one that will allow the company's management enough space to manage, without trying to oversee every single decision. If a major investor is always trying to supervise every detail, and control every decision no matter how small, the support will not seem particularly friendly – nor will it be that helpful.

A building with companionship is always better than a lonely building in the middle of nowhere. However, if a small building is flanked by skyscrapers on both sides, the effect will be one of being squeezed, rather than one of friendly protection. Such a building no longer has a good and nourishing location, because the Yin and Yang (being protected and protecting) of the relationship are unbalanced.

The right features, in the right scale, of the right quality, and the right quantity, with a good balance of yin and yang: these are the keys to good Feng Shui. To understand this fully, and be able to use these tools, is more than philosophy or science; it is an art, which requires not only the cultivation various skills, but long experience that helps provide the basis for a refined intuition. Only thus can one begin to master the art of Feng Shui.

Genuine Ch'i

CHAPTER 5

Ch'i: The Breath of Nature

In the hundreds of volumes of Feng Shui lore, accumulated over thousands of years, the primary discussion is of the landscape, the nature of its features, and their implications. However, at the same time, there is one theme that ties it all together: that is the concept of ch'i.

What is ch'i? Literally thousands of commentaries discuss this point, each with its own point of view. In Chinese metaphysics, ch'i is the very essence or element that composes the whole universe (as we briefly discussed in Chapter 2). All forms, all manifestations, come from ch'i. Without ch'i, there would be no universe. Once the universe appears, all its transformations and developments are nothing but the transformations between ch'i and form.

In a way, every form is not only created by ch'i, but still contains the ch'i that created it. If there is ch'i, there is life. When there is no ch'i, living beings die and material forms disintegrate. In Feng Shui, "good" Feng Shui refers to a place that has an abundance of ch'i. Since ch'i has neither form nor image, ancient Feng Shui masters learned to trace the presence of ch'i indirectly, through different landscape configurations – just as one can see the presence of the wind from the bending of the trees.

In ancient times, people who studied Feng Shui often traveled as widely as possible, studying configurations of mountains and bodies of water, tasting the water, checking the soil, and smelling the air, and observed the aura of the landscape, searching for places where ch'i was abundant.

This was called "searching for the dragon," since the dragon, the living mountain, is an image of the manifestation of ch'i. There is a saying: "Where there is ch'i there is life; where there is no ch'i there is death." Nowadays, people often translate "ch'i" as "vital energy" or "life breath." This expresses some aspects of ch'i, but does not fully express its metaphysical meaning.

As the Feng Shui classics say, "Form defines ch'i, and ch'i manifests through form." In practice, this means that the form of the four landscape features expresses the movement, the flow, and coagulation of ch'i. Ch'i adheres to the land and follows the movement of the dragon. When one sees the momentum of the mountain or dragon, one sees the movement of ch'i. The guardian hills protect the flow of ch'i until it meets the water, where it becomes confined. Where yin and yang meet, the energy coagulates.

One of the most important Feng Shui classics, the *Book of Burials,* by Kuo P'u (276-324 AD), says: "Ch'i rides with the wind, is dissipated by wind, and is confined by water. Hence ancient people sought places where ch'i collected and did not dissipate, where its momentum was held by the water." This is why "wind" and "water" became the terms used to name the flow of earth energy. They represent the most dynamic and changeable forces in the world; they represent the ever-changing flow of manifestation, searching for dynamic balance.

Wind and water, for our planet, are just like blood and breath in the human body. A strong, healthy body requires normal, strong respiration and good circulation. If the breath is short and weak, there is not enough oxygen to nourish the body. If blood flow is

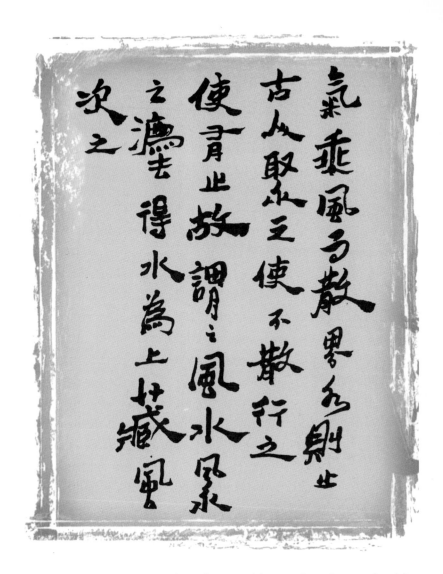

气乘風則散界水則止古人聚之使不散行之使有止故謂之風水聚水之濾去得水為上藏風次之

"Ch'i rides with the wind, is dissipated by wind, and is confined by water. Hence ancient people sought places where ch'i collected and did not dissipate, where its momentum was held by the water. This is why Feng Shui is called Wind and Water; however, the water factor is more important than the wind factor."
— FROM THE BOOK OF BURIALS

too weak or too strong, it can damage the health of the body. In traditional Chinese medicine, a great deal can be told from the respiration and the pulse. One of the key methods of diagnosis is taking the pulse. An experienced doctor can check whether a pulse is too strong, too weak, too stagnant, too slippery, too superficial, too deep, too fast, or too slow. There are twenty-eight basic patterns, which manifest in hundreds of combinations.

Similarly, the Feng Shui master checks the energy of the land by assessing the qualities of each feature of the landscape. The art of doing this is very sophisticated, but it all boils down to assessing Yin-Yang balance, just as the art of taking the pulse in medicine boils down to assessing the balance between opposite qualities.

In a particular landscape, it might be that there is no protection for the ch'i flow; it moves quickly, and dissipates quickly, like wind over an endless prairie. Or it might be like a place surrounded by mountains, where the center is very stagnant, and there is no good ch'i flow. So when we talk about ch'i we have to always think in terms of the form through which it manifests. Form not only defines the amount of ch'i, but also the nature of its flow.

As we have discussed, the concept of form can apply to any scale: landscape, city, house, and so on. Naturally, a house, like a landscape, also has the four basic features, and the form of a house defines the energy of the house.

To demonstrate this point, let's take a simple example. Look at diagram 5.1. Figure A is circular; figure B is square.

When you look at these forms, do you have different reactions? Most likely, you will feel a difference between them, though you may not be able to say clearly what it is. These forms have a physiological or psychological impact, below or beyond the level

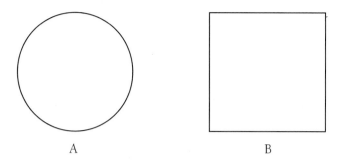

Diagram 5.1   *Circle and Square*

of ordinary awareness. In other words, these forms each manifest or present a different, characteristic kind of ch'i.

If this is real to you, think about three-dimensional objects, like a cube or sphere. Their impact is even more definite. Now think of ordinary surroundings, inside or outside a house. There are literally thousands of forms projecting energy to you, affecting you. Each one presents a different kind of energy, and all these impulses of energy are held within the general structure of the place.

When we say that we are where we live, this means that we are closely affected by our environments – the forms that surround us, and the ch'i that manifests through those forms.

How then do we know which kinds of forms present benefi-cial energy, and which do not? We have to look back to what nature presents to us. All the Feng Shui classics describe different landscapes – real places and real phenomena, not theoretical constructions. Underneath all these real cases, people came to understand that there is a single pattern: the more closely the principles of yin and yang are followed, the better the energy is.

In many modern Feng Shui manuals, people use the term "ch'i" loosely – giving rise to such terms as "bad ch'i," "killing ch'i," "violent ch'i," or "dead ch'i," as though ch'i could be either good or bad. This is a misunderstanding, deriving from a casual way of speaking. When people say that a place has "dead ch'i," what they are often talking about is a place without any ch'i. When people say a place has "killing ch'i," they often simply mean that the flow is excessively strong, or strongly unbalanced.

Ch'i, in fact, is simply present in everything that exists. The total amount does not increase or decrease. However, through different forms of land or structures, it can manifest differently – as coagulation in one place, and flow in another. From a Feng Shui point of view, the important thing is to allow it to flow, and to collect. Ch'i is like sunshine; it is always there. On a cloudy day, or when one draws the blinds, there is still sunshine, but it is blocked. If the sunshine weren't there, it could not be created, or drawn to the place.

If a place is alive, it means that the place has a good, or smooth, flow of ch'i, one that nourishes the land. Small children can jump and run the whole day, without getting tired. They have an abundance of ch'i. When we see old people walking slowly, bent forward, we say they do not have much ch'i. What happened to their ch'i? The ch'i in the world around them is abundant as ever. But adults have many mental blocks: stress, emotions, and so on. All work together to obstruct the flow of ch'i. Babies have few mental and physical blockages. When they are hungry or wet, they cry. When they are comfortable, they smile. There is no interference from attitudes or ideas about what they should or should not do. Babies have supple muscles, fewer polluting chemicals to block energy flow, and less tension and stress. But as they grow into adults, they absorb more pollutants and artificial substances, thus accumulating physical blockages.

The same thing is true of a house or a landscape. A place with fewer blockages will have more abundant energy. This may still seem very abstract, but it is important to have the right perspective at the beginning. In later chapters, we will present more concrete examples.

There are three ways to detect whether a place has good Feng Shui or good ch'i. First, we can perceive it directly. Second, we can study how the energy has manifested in the past. Third, we can study the Feng Shui classics and learn to apply their principles.

People who are very intuitive can follow their own feelings. The problem here is that we are often not able to detect our intuitions; it is too easy to be sidetracked by pre-existing ideas or values, and miss our immediate, intuitive responses. Even those who are very intuitive can still get only general feelings; without having learned a framework of ideas, they cannot communicate this feeling in specific terms.

We can also examine the history of a place to see how the energy has been manifesting. Good Feng Shui will manifest as good ch'i flow, leading to a good life for the people who live there. If a city or place is very prosperous, it is clear that it has good Feng Shui. If a house has been occupied by people who have become successful and healthy, and have developed good relationships while living there, we can be pretty sure that the place has good Feng Shui. But if you do not know the history of a place, you might not be able to use this kind of clue to assess the nature of its ch'i. And this method cannot be used with new houses or other buildings.

For people who seriously want to study Feng Shui, one of the best ways to get a grasp of it is to start with the classical teachings. Once that knowledge is mastered, and enhanced by experience, one will also develop an intuitive sense. But the problem is that, although there are many new books currently available, it is not easy to tell which ones are reliable. It is always necessary to refer back to the basic concepts of yin-yang and five element theory, which are the backbone of the classical tradition.

The balance of yin and yang is an aspect of natural law that describes static configurations. Five element theory is also the aspect of natural law describing dynamic transformations. Since the five elements each have their corresponding forms, if the forms are elementally compatible, they make up a good building. When they are not, the building is disorganized.

Forms are manifestations of the energies of the activities that are suited to them. In the tables in Chapter 2 that deal with the Five Element Theory, we have said that the long shape is connected with the Wood element, that square shapes are links with the Earth element, round with Metal, triangle with Fire, and irregular forms with Water. Since form manifests ch'i, these forms can be said to be manifesting the ch'i of the element with which they are connected. These forms represent the ch'i of expansion, of stability, of coagulation, of radiation, and of penetration, respectively. Each represents a particular mode of transformation and the energy behind that mode.

This is why business buildings tend to be tall (linked to the Wood element), indicating expansion and growth. Warehouses tend to be stable coagulations (Earth), and thus to be low and square. Triangular buildings are rare, since triangles belong to Fire, which is easily out of control and chaotic, and such buildings manifest the kind of activities that would tend to consume them. Triangular buildings are seldom successful. Water usually manifests in large complexes of buildings – most often in the kind of complex of structures one sees in a vacation resort, where one can move freely and easily, and not be confined.

A mosque, with its square base and round dome, is an instance of Earth nourishing Metal. Cathedrals are a combination of Wood and Fire: Wood creates Fire, and these forms are also compatible. But a tall building with a circular top would be incompatible, because Metal and Wood are in conflict. (We talk about this in more detail in Chapter 8.)

We have discussed the four features of the landscape – the dragon, energy spot, guardian, and water – as basic tools for evaluating the quality of a place. But underlying these features are the yin-yang and five element theory, which must be understood for effective energy design. These, after all, are the keys to the patterns of natural process. It is being in harmony with natural processes that allows one to lead a good life.

We have seen what this means in general. In the next chapter, we will look at a specific, more concrete example.

福地福人居

Good is the place

where good people live.

CHAPTER 6

In Search of an Ideal House

Good Feng Shui can be analyzed in terms of the four features we have already discussed, using yin-yang principle and five element theory as the guidelines.

But for many readers, this will still be somewhat abstract and hard to apply. In this chapter, we would like to get more specific, and use a residential house as an example to bring these points into focus.

There are four criteria that are essential for any house to be a good one. The house should have a good location, a wholesome form, a smooth ch'i flow, and a good feeling. This may seem like common sense – and, after all, Feng Shui is very much in line with common sense, a sense that is shared by everyone, that is universal, and that follows natural patterns – even though in modern times common sense seems to have become a scarce commodity. Nowadays we often find that we have turned away from our own inner perceptions and have come to rely heavily on outside opinions from specialists and so-called experts. We actually have to get back to what our inner senses already tell us.

GOOD LOCATION

What makes a good location? A good location is one with a complete, balanced complement of the four Feng Shui features. Flat ground is better than a steep hillside; a mountain-top or a valley-bottom will not be as good as a place in some less extreme location between them. A place on a busy street with fast traffic is not balanced; neither is a place that is remote and isolated. A more or less homogeneous and harmonious neighborhood is better than a jumbled, miscellaneous one or a monotonously identical one.

Of course, a good location is most often in a more prosperous neighborhood – though this is not always the case. For a good residence, the neighborhood has to be suitable for a dwelling – and this means that it might be very different from the kind of neighborhood that would be good for a business. Even if a neighborhood has a balanced environment in general, to be suitable for you it also has to be in balance with your lifestyle.

When people turn to their common sense, they do understand what makes a location a good one. A good house should be readily accessible to a road, but not have heavy traffic. It will have a big open space or yard in front, making it easy to get to. The neighboring houses will be similar and compatible; it will not be squeezed between oppressively big buildings, or isolated. It will sit on more or less flat ground; if it is on a hill, the hill will be gentle, and will rise behind the house, so that there will be an open, spacious area in front of the house. It will be a place where the earth has sufficient energy to nourish plants and trees.

WHOLESOME FORM

A house should have a wholesome form. "Wholesome" means complete, full, and regular – in contrast to fragmented, choppy or irregular, or very strange or bizarre. The external form of a house should appear to be complete and amiable. The floor plan should not be too fragmented or broken up, nor should there be many zigzag or cutting structures. The purest forms are the square and the circle, representing pure yin and pure yang, respectively. Both forms are very wholesome. The more a form deviates from them, the less wholesome it is. Most examples of beautiful and great architecture, throughout history, East and West, are skilled combinations of these two forms, pure and balanced. Even buildings with very ornate designs still largely adhere to these basic forms underneath their ornament.

For a residence, the ideal structural form is basically square (Yin), or somewhat rectangular, since a residence is a place for rest and quiet. Round structural forms, being more dynamic, are better for places like sports arenas. From the outside, it should be clear that the house has a stable foundation and structure. The inside floor plan for each room should also stay with square or rectangular forms. In fact, historically, most houses are built along these lines. It is only nowadays that houses have come to be increasingly fragmented and irregular, perhaps reflecting the chaotic energy of the modern world.

Wholesome forms bring forth wholesome energy. Chaotic and fragmented forms reinforce chaotic energy. Behind this modern burst of chaotic forms is a technology that has outrun talent, that allows for, and even demands, a greatly increased range of creativity; but this technology itself cannot make people more creative. As a result, people often take difference to be a sign of creativity, and think that a design is better to the extent that it is unlike anything that has been done before – no matter how uncomfortable it may be to see or to live in. Any room with too many angles, or with many triangular or other strange forms, should be avoided.

The triangle is the least wholesome structural form, and should be avoided as much as possible. No triangular building is good, either as a residence or as a business. But this should not be taken as a criticism of triangular roofs: the roof is only one feature, and form is assessed from the structure as a whole.

An A-frame building is a special case. They are often seen in cold regions, especially ski resorts. They are successful as vacation homes, because vacationers do not need them to nourish long-term, stable activities, and they are successful in cold, snowy situations, where the Fire configuration counteracts the effects of excessive cold and moisture. In either case, they are at best temporary dwellings.

Many new houses have such features as uneven ceilings or uneven floors (sunken living rooms are a good example). These attempts to create a sense of greater space, or to define different spaces, bring forth even greater negative factors. In trying to fix a problem, they bring forth other problems.

SMOOTH CH'I ENERGY FLOW

A good house should also have a smooth ch'i energy flow. Outside, this manifests as the flow of traffic: the house should be easily accessible, but should not be in the middle of heavy traffic. But this is also relevant to the internal structure of the house. A house should have clear and clean connections between the rooms. The movement of energy inside the house should not be too fast or too slow. In a house that is too open, with poorly defined spaces, the flow of ch'i is too fast. If there is a big window immediately facing the door, so that you immediately see the outside as soon as you enter – as though you had no sooner entered the house than you had already left it – the energy flow is also too fast. On the other hand, if a house is too partitioned, and if the passageways turn too much, forming a maze, then the energy flow is too slow. There will be rooms to which the energy does not connect, and there will be many "dead" rooms in the house.

A space that is too open or a flow that is too fast is like diarrhea; a house where the flow is too slow is like constipation. Neither is good. An ideal arrangement is that once you enter a house, you have a good mental picture of how it is laid out, even though you will not be able to see everything at one glance. In a house with good ch'i flow, each room will have a good connection with any other room, even if the connection is not direct. When all the rooms are connected well, all the people who live there are connected well.

GOOD FEELING

A good house should also make you feel good. Again, this is common sense, but it is worth pointing out. People have immediate responses to places: a place may feel comfortable or uncomfortable, warm or cold. Everyone has experienced this: in some houses people naturally gather in a living room; in others they naturally gather in a kitchen or family room. This is a natural response to the spatial energy of the house, and to the particular rooms. If people just attend to the kind of response that leads people to gravitate to one place rather than another, they can tell if the energy of the place is good or not.

However, people are often easily distracted by pre-existing preferences or by unusual features in the house – marble floors in the bathroom, an extra-large kitchen, or other features that are pleasing to an individual's taste. These features often sidetrack people, and keep them from seeing – or sensing – the whole picture.

Generally speaking, if the first three criteria that we have mentioned as essential for a good house are satisfied, the house will probably have a good feeling as well. There are, however, special cases in which people feel that a house has "bad vibes" or "bad energy." Sometimes this is related to residual thought-forms that remain in the house from a previous owner or from previous events. For example, if a mortuary is converted into a house, even after a long time there can still be traces of odd energy. The same thing is true for prisons – though such cases are actually rather rare.

These four criteria (good location, wholesome form, smooth energy flow, and good feeling) are very general, but they are fundamental. It is important to approach the subject first from the general viewpoint, rather than from specific rules. Once the general approach has been understood, we can do quite a bit of fine-tuning by means of more specific rules. But if one just starts from a collection of rules, one will not know the context for their use, and it will be impossible to use them well.

As we pointed out in the last chapter, there are three approaches to assessing the qualities of a place. One can use intuition, or one can study the effects of the place on its inhabitants, or one can analyze it through the basic concepts of Yin and Yang and the Five Element theory. Careful study will provide eventual understanding. Intuition itself may lead us to the right feeling, but may not show us the right way to act on it.

It is by following the traditional method – learning the systematic knowledge and mastering it – that one can develop one's intuition. A great Feng Shui master may not easily tell whether his understanding of the nature of a place comes from intuition or from knowledge. When one has truly mastered an art, intuition and knowledge become one thing, one organ of perception and understanding.

Now that we have introduced these general principles, we can go on to took at more specific requirements for particular kinds of rooms, and how to work with these requirements when designing a house and the rooms within it.

氣固於形形全則氣全

Form defines energy.

If form is wholesome, energy is wholesome.

Close-Up On Interiors:
Key Features

A good house should be in a good location, have a wholesome form, provide good ch'i flow, and make you feel good – as we discussed in the last chapter. But now let us look at some key individual features within the house.

Houses often have a living room, bedrooms, a family room, kitchen, dining room, study, bathroom, storage areas, garage, all connected by hallways or staircases. In this chapter, we will discuss the key features of the house: the main entrance, the bedroom, and the kitchen.

The entrance is the face of the house, the link between the outside (yang) and the inside (yin). It is the major passageway for ch'i flow. It represents the image, the personality, or character of the house, and is the primary source of ch'i input and flow for the house. This is why it is so important.

Most people spend about a third of their lives asleep – in the bedroom. So the bedroom obviously has a major impact on human life, even though that impact is usually not something of which people are consciously aware.

The kitchen is the source of food, and many important activities take place there. Because of this, it is another key feature of the house.

(The other rooms will not be discussed in this book: they will be dealt with in full detail in *Feng Shui in Interior Space and Design,* the second book in this series.)

THE MAIN ENTRANCE

There is an old Feng Shui saying: "The main entrance is worth a thousand pounds of gold; the rest of the house is worth only four ounces." This shows how important ancient Feng Shui masters thought the main entrance to be.

Most of the time, the main entrance is the front door of the house. The main door is the center that coordinates the four features: it is in a pivotal position, because the position and direction of the door determine the relationship of the house (the energy spot) with its surroundings – the mountain, guardians, and water features of the place. The door of a house is like the face of a person. It is the place from which you see the world, and the place through which the world recognizes you. This is why it is important for the door to be clearly noticeable, and to stand out – and not be hidden in a corner. In the same way, it is important for a person to have enough confidence to face the world, instead of shying away from it. After all, in a sense, you are the house, and the house reflects you.

In classical buildings, the entrance is always at the center, just as the eyes, nose, and mouth are at the center of a face. In this way, the left (yang) and right (yin) sides are balanced. (The left side of the house, when you stand in the door looking out, is masculine or yang; the right side is feminine or yin.) If the door is located all the way to one side or the other, either the yin or the yang quality will predominate.

The size of the door should be proportional to the size of the house. A small house should not have too big a door, nor should a large house have too small a door. From the door looking outward, you should face an open, clear, and clean environment – without piled-up debris, dead trees, oddly shaped objects, or overgrown tree branches or vegetation blocking the view. There is a Feng Shui saying that if, whenever you go out the door, the front area is clear and smooth, then your day will go smoothly and peacefully.

A common rule found in many Feng Shui texts is that there should not be a tree (or in modern times a telephone pole) in front of the door. The idea behind this to avoid the blockage of ch'i flow, since the door is the main passageway through which ch'i flows into the house from the outside. However, it is important to understand that this depends on scale, and not to apply the rule blindly or rigidly. A small tree in front of a house probably does not block the flow – nor does a large tree far away from the house. A telephone pole right in front of the door may not be desirable, but a telephone pole across the street will not have a noticeable negative effect.

Similarly, as soon as you go in the front door, there should be a nice, open space, providing a good transition from outside (yang) to inside (yin). The space should feel inviting. If, instead, you immediately face a wall that forces you to turn when you come in, or you face a high staircase, the effect is less inviting. It is farther from the ideal, because there is no space to hold the ch'i, and no buffer zone to provide a smooth transition.

Right after the entrance, the transitional space should be simple and elegant, not busy and complicated. Since this area is immediately adjacent to the outside, which is yang, the inside should be well lit. It should not create too dramatic a shift from yang to yin.

Nowadays, many people use the garage to enter the house, making the garage door the main entrance. When the garage door is in front, it is often aligned with the main door, preserving the coordination of features; the relationships with mountain, guardian hills, and water do not change much. However, there are also many houses with kitchen and parking in the back, so that the back door becomes the primary entrance. This tends to shift the relationship between the mountain, guardian hills, and water. The Feng Shui of such a house should be evaluated by taking the back door as the main entrance.

Many American houses have a great view and an impressive front door, but people often go in and out via the back door. The impressive view in front may present an excellent coordination of the four features, but if the back entrance is used as the main entrance, all the effects of the configuration change, and its benefits may be lost.

THE BEDROOM

People spend about one third of their lives asleep, so the Feng Shui of the bedroom is naturally very important. It affects all aspects of the lives of those who sleep there, but especially matters of health and relationship.

The most important thing in a bedroom is the positioning of the bed. In Chapter 4, we have already discussed some aspects of ideal bedroom arrangement. The bed should lean against a solid wall, with no window directly behind or above the bed. There should be no door or passageway on either side of the bed. There should be no passageway directly in front of the bed. The door or passageway into the bedroom should be diagonally in front of the bed, so that it is clearly seen from the bed, but not directly facing it.

These points are derived from the ideal model of the four features, in which the mountain or support is behind, the protecting guardian hills are on either side, and there is smooth water flow in front.

The bedroom is a room for rest, for replenishing your energy. Therefore, it is not an active, dynamic, yang room; it is a yin room (in contrast to the living room, which is the most yang room). Thus, it is good to avoid too many yang elements or factors: too many or too large windows, too much light, too many circular shapes in the room, too bright colors, too complicated or ornate furniture, and so on.

The furniture and its arrangement should be simple and wholesome, so there will not be too much choppiness, fragmentation, or clutter in the space.

The relative size of the bedroom is also important. In modern times, the bedrooms in new houses tend to be bigger and bigger. Sometimes even the bathroom and closet are just as big as the bedroom. The bedroom provides a space to house and support human beings; at the same time, human beings also support and nourish the room (and the house) through their own energy. It is common knowledge that a vacant, unoccupied house tends to deteriorate faster than an occupied house. This is because the lack of human energy in an empty house makes it undernourished, so it naturally tends to deteriorate more quickly. This is why a long-empty house feels cold. This is not a matter of the temperature of the house, but of the lack of ch'i in the house. As we said in Chapter 2, the universe is nothing but ch'i and form, with form created by ch'i and sustained by ch'i. When ch'i is depleted, form tends to disintegrate.

Following this logic, a larger bedroom will naturally require more energy to fill. Either people will be depleted of more energy to sustain the place, or the average energy of the house will be less. The consequence of this decrease in ch'i will be less ch'i for the people, who will be more likely to be tired, fatigued, depressed, or insomniac. This can lead to chronic diseases.

Large bathrooms or closets connected to the bedroom will amplify or compound the negative effect, since even more space will have to be supported by the energy of those who live there. Ideally, in this case, there would be a door that would separate the two spaces.

On the other hand, if a bedroom is too small this will also not be ideal, since the ch'i will not have a good flow and will tend to stagnate. But if one has to choose between the two mistakes, it is better for the bedroom to be too small than to be too large.

A large window over or behind the bed does not allow the energy to coagulate in the bed and nourish the people who sleep there. In addition to health problems, it will also tend to have a negative impact on the relationship of the couple who sleeps there. In such a situation, it is better to wall up the window. Placing a large painting over it to block it will do the job.

How these mistakes will affect health and relationships is really proportional to the size of the problem. A small transom window above the bed may not have a negative effect. A window on the side, rather than directly behind the bed, will not have that much negative effect either.

Basically, if the bed has a solid wall behind it, and the bedroom has adequate natural light, and adequate size and ventilation, you will probably have good sleep and good health.

THE KITCHEN

The kitchen is the source of food; people gather there for meals and other activities. It is one of the most dynamic places in the house. It affects the health, relationships, and economy of the household.

The two most important features of the kitchen are the stove and the faucet: fire, the yang factor, and water, the yin factor. These are metaphors for the masculine and feminine energies.

Remember that when we talked about water and mountain in Chapter 3, we said that the water was yang and the mountain was yin. But in situations where water is contrasted with fire, water is yin and fire is yang. It is important to remember that yin and yang are not inherent properties of things, but the qualities that they have in their relationships with other things.

The ideal arrangement for the stove and the water source is the traditional arrangement in which stove and sink form a 90-degree angle, as shown in diagram 7.1, where there is a window behind the sink and a solid wall behind the stove.

The stove is Fire, and thus linked with consumption and the spending of money. People like to be able to control how they spend money. Control, and stability, are linked with the mountain feature. Here, the wall behind the stove is the Mountain. This is why a solid wall behind the stove is necessary, so that there can be control over the rate of spending of family or household resources, in other words, good budgetary control. When the stove is not well supported, people will tend to have frequent surprise expenditures. It does not have anything to do with one's intrinsic wealth – just with the tendency for surprise items to appear in the budget.

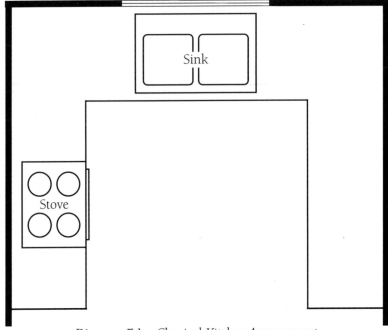

Diagram 7.1 *Classical Kitchen Arrangement*

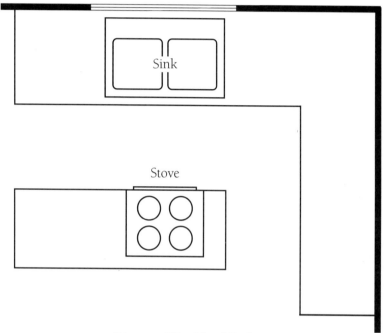

Diagram 7.2   *Island Kitchen*

The ninety-degree relationship of the sink and stove also, of course, makes more ergonomic sense for anyone cooking. Nowadays, however, it is fashionable to have an "island kitchen," in which the stove is placed on an island, as shown in diagram 7.2.

In such a case, the stove has no support; nor does it have any protection on the sides. It will be more difficult to have real control of the household budget. In an island kitchen, too, it is likely that Water and Fire will confront each other. As we have mentioned, they are metaphors for female and male energy, and this confrontation will make it more challenging to maintain a good relationship between female and male in the household.

If this sort of mistake is coupled with a bedroom in which there is a window behind the bed, one can almost be sure that the relationship of a couple living in such a house will be less harmonious – if it survives at all.

The question of the ideal placement of oven, refrigerator, microwave, dishwashers, and other gadgets is a secondary matter. The most important thing is to take care of the most important matters first. When stove and sink are correctly positioned, the rest of the features can be filled in.

Similarly, in dealing with the bedroom we discussed the most important feature – the bed – and not the vanity or other items. It is important not to get stuck arranging small details and forget the larger ones – or worse, in working on smaller matters, to undermine the more important ones.

As we said before, the kitchen is a yang room (more yang than the bedroom but less yang than the living room). Therefore, it is ideal to have a window behind the sink, as most conventional kitchens do. This makes the room more yang.

In this chapter, we have said a lot about what is good and what is not. These points and ideal arrangements are all taken from the basic Feng Shui model, and illustrate how it is applied.

The chances are that the better these patterns are followed, the more one will be in harmony with nature, and the less one will suffer negative consequences. Although we often say that certain things affect either health, money, or relationship, it is really not possible to treat these factors in isolation. It is always necessary to look at them in the context of the whole house when making an evaluation. If there is a conflict or mistake in the bedroom, but the house as a whole is very wholesome and the energy is very good, the effects of the mistake may not manifest, since they can be mollified by the general qualities of the house. A challenged relationship might be able to survive by making adjustments supported by other good features of the house. But if the form and flow are not good for the house as a whole, a confrontation of Water and Fire alone might be linked to an angry divorce or bad fights. This is why rules should not be taken rigidly or in isolation; one should never take one's eye away from the whole picture.

If you keep the whole picture in mind, you will be able to see that many of the points mentioned here will be validated through your own experiences and observations, and you will come to understand how to avoid unbalanced configurations and their consequences.

人法地　地法天　天法道　道法自然

Mankind follows Earth.

Earth follows Heaven.

Heaven follows Tao.

And Tao follows the ways of Nature.

CHAPTER 8

Design Principles

" Form defines energy, and energy manifests through form." When we say that we are affected by the environment, we mean that we are affected by forms. There are forms at every scale: large-scale landscape, city layout, neighborhood, the structure of a house, the floor plan and furniture, and patterns of design and decoration. Large scale or small, three-dimensional or two-dimensional or even one-dimensional, all forms emanate energy that affects us.

As we mentioned in Chapter 5, just by looking at the simple diagrams of a square and circle (see diagram 5.1) we can realize that we have different responses, physiological and psychological, to their different structures. This suggests that the drawings emanate different kinds of energies that connect with us and affect us.

If a simple drawing has such an effect, then think of the impact of the large, complex forms surrounding us. The energy that emanates from forms we might call "form energy," or we could, as the ancient Chinese did, call it ch'i. This energy is still to be defined and understood. Nevertheless, for thousands of years, in China and around the world, knowingly and unknowingly, people have responded to its influence, and intuitively designed their environments to take the impact of this energy into account.

The fundamental basis of all this is the structure of natural law – yin-yang and five element theory – discussed in Chapter 2. These are regarded as the highest order of design principles.

Colors, forms, shapes, patterns, size, variety – these design elements must be seen in the context of the yin-yang and five element point of view. It is best to begin with the highest-order principles to balance the individual elements for particular purposes and functions.

Similarly, in Chinese medicine, there are eight major diagnostic types. However, the first step in making a diagnosis is to decide whether the patient's condition is of the yin or yang variety. Once this is decided, a more particular diagnosis can be sought. The big picture comes first.

The same thing is true of environmental design. For example, if you want to create an office space that is more stimulating and energetic, you will want to use more yang elements in the design, such as warmer colors, more vertical lines and patterns, more light, and more space. To design a quiet and tranquil environment, use more yin elements, such as cooler colors, horizontal lines and patterns, more partitions for privacy, and so on. Naturally, you would not want to go to extremes in either case; remember that in the T'ai Chi diagram there is always yang in yin and yin in yang.

Strictly vertical lines are too yang and can also be boring. If you superimpose the images of trees (vertical) or floral patterns, you will bring some yin to yang, and soften the effect. Strictly horizontal lines are too yin and are also boring, and are better replaced by horizontal waving lines, which introduce some dynamic (yang) effects (see diagrams 8.1 and 8.2).

If we are to design a fast-food restaurant, where people are supposed to eat and leave in a relatively short time, the traffic flow should be fast (i.e., yang), so we need to implement more yang elements in the design: more windows, a well-lit, spacious

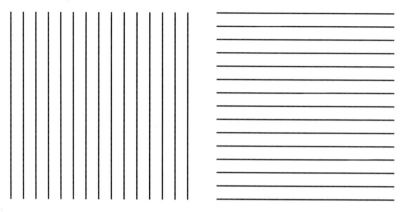

Pure Yang Pattern   Pure Yin Pattern

Diagram 8.1   *Abstract Vertical and Horizontal Patterns*

Predominantly Yang Pattern   Predominantly Yin Pattern

Diagram 8.2   *Natural Vertical and Horizontal Patterns*

place, light or bright colors, simple design, and some round or rounded tables.

A fancier, more leisurely dining environment, where people are intending to spend more time to enjoy the food and atmosphere, for serious formal gatherings or romantic dining, requires a slower (more yin) traffic flow. The design should involve more yin elements: more defined space, with more partitions to provide privacy, house plants, dimmer light, and square or rectangular tables.

In both cases, it is important not to go to extremes. If the fast-food restaurant is too yang – too many windows, totally open space, no spatial definition – then people might find the flow too fast for comfort even for a short time. Similarly, for a formal restaurant, an exclusively yin design could produce stagnation, which would make people feel suffocated or depressed, and this also is not ideal.

For structures, as mentioned in Chapter 6, wholesomeness of form is essential. But it is also important to identify the nature of the building, and apply yin and yang principles. A sports arena is active, public, exciting, and thus requires yang elements, especially a circular form. For a private residence, a square design and yin elements are much more appropriate. Again, however, in either case, the aim is to achieve the right balance, rather than to go to extremes.

All great buildings, anywhere in the world, show clear applications of the principles of wholesome form and the balance of yin and yang. The square or rectangular base of cathedrals is usually balanced by arches, and by rounded stained-glass windows. The beautiful Moslem mosques have a square base and a round, domed top, which is a wholesome balance of yin and yang elements.

Yin-yang balance does not mean that the two elements should be equal. Much depends on the nature of the structure. Yin-yang balance applies not only to structure or environment; it also has to do with the people who live there. After all, the building only means something in relation to the people.

In this context, the people are yang and the house is yin, since the people form the dynamic component and the house forms the stable component in the relationship. The balance between the building and the people is essential. An active young couple expecting to have several children requires a different environment than an older, retired couple who may wish to enjoy their retirement without much social entanglement. They will require different environments to suit their lifestyles. The size of the house and the number of people living there should also be in balance. The more people, the larger the house; the fewer people, the smaller the house. This seems like a simple concept, and a common sense one. Yet vanity, ego, and false pride often drive people to make the wrong choices, to desire a house larger than they need as a way to show their status, or to compensate for some lack that they feel. This outer imbalance reflects an imbalance of the heart, since all outward manifestations are reflections of inner conditions.

In any environmental or structural design, on any scale, there are literally hundreds of elements, of difference scales of importance, that must be considered. One should always begin at the highest level, and from there go to the details. From the level of energy to that of the manifestation of the whole form to the specifics and details. People often focus on details and miss the big picture; they mistakenly try to take care of a single tree and forget the whole forest.

Another important aspect of natural law is captured by five element theory. This complements the yin-yang theory, by expressing the mechanisms of transformation that occur throughout the universe and also the transforming manifestations of energy. Like yin-yang theory, five element theory applies to all aspects of human life – medicine, management, government affairs, even military strategy. (Why did Napoleon march into Moscow without much difficulty, but suffer defeat even after occupying Moscow? Why did the Sino-Japanese War go the way it did? This can be understood by analysis based on the five element theory.)

In house and building design, five element theory is useful for interpreting design dynamics, since all forms and colors have their connections with the five elements. (See diagram 2.2.) Long and tall forms relate to Wood, triangles relate to Fire, square forms to Earth, round forms to Metal, and irregular forms to Water.

The tall (Wood) Catholic cathedral with pointed (Fire) tops is a good combination: Wood enhances the Fire element (see diagram 2.2). If the top of such a tall building is replaced by a round or half-circular form (Metal), it would look odd, since Metal and Wood are in conflict. The Moslem mosque, with a square (Earth) base and a round (Metal) top is a good combination, since Earth nourishes Metal.

Such applications and interpretations can apply to aspects beyond form and color. Diagram 2.2 shows the nourishing and restraining relationships between the elements. In design work, there are times when one wants to use the nourishing relationship to foster harmony; there are also times when one can use the restraining relationship to express conflict for particular purposes. For example, red (Fire) and black (Water) are in conflict – but this conflict can focus the attention and make the design stand out, a method often used in graphic design.

One of the most successful restaurants, MacDonald's, has a very good logo. The golden yellow arch with a rectangular red base demands a closer analysis. The arch, a circular (Yang) form, with a square (Yin) on the bottom, is appropriately arranged, since Yang (heaven) is above and Yin (earth) is below. Yellow (Earth) and Red (Fire) complement each other: Fire creates Earth. Earth is associated with the stomach, and Fire with the heart (mind). Therefore, this design appeals to people's stomachs (appetite) and desires (heart): a perfect fit for a fast-food restaurant. Whoever designed this logo probably had no idea about yin-yang and five element theory, but his intuition naturally connected with universal laws, which are what yin-yang and five element theory express. As a matter of fact, since all restaurants need to appeal to appetite and desire, restaurant signs should all incorporate some yellow and red colors.

From a five element point of view, a triangle is linked with Fire, often associated with conflict, chaos, and violence. This form must be used with great care. This can be seen wherever there are city blocks with triangular shapes. Such blocks are usually more plagued with conflict than others. Triangular buildings usually do not bring success, no matter what the business or the management team.

In Chapter 3, we mentioned the form of the Indian subcontinent. It is the triangular form of the subcontinent which is linked to the clashing languages, cultures, and religions, that prevents the country from becoming unified and developing a stronger international presence.

In any business, as with all other human activities, there are (as we have already mentioned) three elements: Heaven (time), People, and Earth (space). If one of these has grave shortcomings, it can be very hard for the other two to compensate. This is why triangles are not good for places, for houses, for layout, or for shapes in particular rooms. Once the space deviates too far from the square or rectangular, there will be a lot of wasted space. This is also true for furniture arrangement.

Many popular Feng Shui manuals often suggest that a desk be put into a corner, thus creating a triangular space behind the desk (see diagram 8.3). In this case, the mountain is no longer parallel with the back. This may not be very serious, but it will nevertheless tend to bring many small troubles or annoyances for people who sit there. Instead, it is better to avoid this

Diagram 8.3   *Diagonal Desk Placement (Not ideal)*

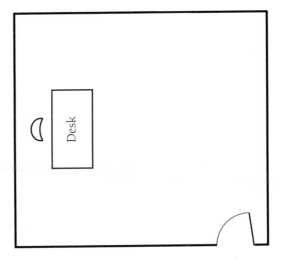

Diagram 8.4   *Parallel Desk Placement (Ideal)*

triangular configuration, and have one's back parallel to a wall, as in diagram 8.4.

It is easy to confirm this right away, by a simple test. Put a desk as in diagram 8.3 or 8.4 and sit there for a few minutes to see which arrangement feels better. Also have people sit across from you, and see how they feel. The differences will be very noticeable.

There are places where triangles are appropriate. In such cases, the triangle should point upward, as in roofs or pyramids, since a triangle pertains to Fire, and is linked with the upward movement of energy.

Feng Shui is not a belief system or religion, nor is it folklore. It is based on natural law; it is universal in its applications. Many of the practices connected with Feng Shui in its originating culture do have parallel connections with natural law (since culture comes from prolonged life experience). It is important to know, however, whether particular practices apply to everyone, or just to members of a regional culture. The best way to determine this is to see whether such Feng Shui practices are in tune with our inner feelings or not.

Some practices and rules are obviously derived from folklore or even superstitions, such as hanging bamboo flutes, emphasizing mirrors and red-colored doors, and so on. These might apply in some settings, but they are not particularly universal. Sometimes people even think that a house designed according to Feng Shui principles must look very "oriental." But the Feng Shui "look" has nothing to do with an "oriental" look.

Feng Shui design must be seen from the energy level rather than from just the physical level. Of course, physical manifestation is required to express the energy. But the key is energy, and the key to the energy level is the balanced interaction of yin and yang, and the mutual coordination of the five elements. Without this, no design is according to Feng Shui principles. With it, even a medieval castle, an Egyptian temple, or a stone circle can be in tune with Feng Shui principles. It is alignment with laws of nature, not particular social customs, that counts.

Ten thousand dharmas

all manifest from the heart.

CHAPTER 9

The Heart of Feng Shui

To live is to create. Every day, we are creating our lives, our ways of living. At every minute, in deciding how to live our lives, we create our living environments. We create our own Feng Shui.

Where is the source of this creation? We don't need to look far: it is here. It is what surrounds us. The source of this creation is in the realm of the universe and it is within us. The quality and scale of the creation, however, depend on how far and how deeply we tap into what is around us – on whatever scale we can reach.

In speaking of the man-made structure environment – design of houses, city blocks, or whole cities – some are orderly and some chaotic; some please us and some do not. Building design, like every other setting, manifests the energy of the groups and individuals who live there – and of the energy and character of the architects, builders, and developers who produced it.

Modern architects tend to avoid following traditional building design. In part, this is due to modern materials and technology, which allow for surprising structures that could not be built before our time. But it is also due to a desire to be known as a creative artist. Some architects are talented and creative; others try to be creative, but are limited by their own talent. The desire to be creative tends to make them design things that are different just for the sake of difference. When the ambition to be creative is not backed up by talent, the creation tends to be chaotic and tends to produce chaos.

People often confuse differentness with creativity. Many artists create very bizarre things in the name of self-expression, but in fact they are simply releasing their own psychic or emotional garbage, rather than using it as compost to nourish true creativity. The artists gain some pleasure and benefit from this release, but to the public it is often just a nuisance. Many trends in modern building can be classed in this category. But who is responsible? Are the architects to blame? Or are they just, like us, shaped by all the energies that surround them?

Some architects who do have talent and skill are often unknowingly used as vehicles to express particular sorts of energy. Every form of energy in the universe finds a vehicle through which to express itself. I. M. Pei's Bank of China building in Hong Kong and Frank O. Gehry's Guggenheim Museum in the city of Bilbao in northern Spain are good examples. The 70-floor Bank of China building, with its square base and four triangles on the top, is a tall, arrogant, and sharply angled building, cutting like a blade into the island of Hong Kong. It offends many Hong Kong residents, especially because they are very sensitive to Feng Shui. People can blame Mr. Pei for this design, but he may simply have been transmitting the arrogant energy from China. Even before Hong Kong returned to China's control in 1997, China was already there. The building was simply a manifestation of that fact, and that overwhelming presence. It is not a matter of whether Mr. Pei should or should not have taken Feng Shui into consideration. If that particular energy or message needed to manifest, it would find its own way to do so, through Mr. Pei or otherwise.

THE HEART OF FENG SHUI   ☯   *101*

The Guggenheim Museum has been controversial since the beginning. It has attracted both praise and criticism; people either love it or hate it. It follows Frank O. Gehry's signature style. Whether we like it or not is not the point. From the Feng Shui point of view, the design is dominated by triangles and waving forms and lines. It is composed of the elements of Fire and Water. It represents conflict, confusion, and chaos. It may well be that this building simply makes a statement for the twentieth century, epitomizing its chaos and confusion. The fact that it is on such a grand scale demands that people pay attention. This is the way it is; it has nothing to do with right or wrong. If this energy did not manifest through this building, it would manifest through other buildings.

Different molds produce different shapes, and different kinds of pipes or vehicles will convey different kinds of energies. Great architects not only have talent, but the sensitivity to allow energy to channel through them in a more integral way. The Jefferson and Lincoln Memorials in the United States are good examples of this. They are not only elegant and beautiful; they also clearly manifest the characters of these two presidents. You can correlate the character of the two buildings with the personalities of the two presidents.

Many of the great structures throughout history have been religious structures – Catholic cathedrals, Moslem mosques, Buddhist temples. Their aim is to glorify or worship God, Heaven, or the Truth. Their architects are able to tap into a higher source of energy, and manifest it. In a sense, we can say that it is God working through the architect. Therefore, the master architects for such grand buildings often dedicate their talent or skill as a vehicle for a higher energy, instead of trying to express their limited or mundane personalities, which are often mixed with pride and ego.

More than frequently, we look at city buildings and see a lack of cohesiveness, a lack of pleasing harmony. When you go to the wilderness – the jungle, the prairie, or steppe – nothing seems incoherent or discordant. Everything seems cohesive, integrated, and harmonious. Some tropical forests literally have three layers of vegetation, in three climate zones, with hundreds of species in any locality. Yet every plant seems to have found its right place.

How often does one see such cohesion and integration in cities or neighborhoods? Instead of beginning the design process from the point of view of the relationship between human beings and nature and natural laws, architects may be focused mainly on their particular buildings; developers focused on maximum return from their developments; city planners more concerned with promoting growth than with controlling it or patterning it. Acting from these limited points of view, they produce chaotic and inharmonious results.

In nature, natural processes or forces will bring about mutual adjustments between organisms. Man-made buildings are not as easy to demolish or reshape. We have to live with their consequences much longer.

Why is nature so different from the human world? Nature follows natural law. Balancing occurs at every moment. There is no ego or pride; there is no resistance to the natural flow. There is no selfishness; therefore the flow goes wherever it needs to. There is no individual pride. There is nothing to be accomplished; thus everything is accomplished naturally.

We human beings are also creators of energy forms. Form creates energy, and energy manifests form. Which comes first is like the question of the chicken and the egg. It does not matter which one is first. From the point of view of the universal law of T'ai Chi, the beginning is an ending and the ending is the beginning. Cause and effect are not fixed in a single sequence. Sometimes the cause is an effect and the effect is actually the cause.

We should begin wherever we can, with whatever opportunity is given to us. Many people are interested in Feng Shui, and study it, with the idea of changing their environments to improve their lives. This desire for a change for the better is already a good start. However, when people focus only on changing the outside factors, they often lose sight of the fact that the inside and outside are not only connected, but inseparable. Inside and outside are like yin and yang: one cannot exist without the other. Feng Shui is beyond being a matter of fundamental principles, or trivial rules, to be applied to our lives. We need to see the whole picture. Outside factors do affect us – but it is the inner transformation that ensures that the outward manifestations will have a lasting effect.

The highest goal of human achievement, as ancient Chinese sages pointed out thousands of years ago, is to follow the Tao. To follow the Tao is to follow the path of nature. To design for prosperity, health, or better relationships, or to collect and arrange gadgets in the hope of attracting fortune and love, are all manipulations of outside factors. It is good to try to improve things – but to rely purely on external factors can create changes that are only temporary. Since everything is a reflection of the heart, the ultimate solution is to bring the heart into balance. The balanced heart is one that can resonate with the universal heart. In this way, one is in harmony with the nature, and at one with the universe.

All design begins with design of the heart. The Tao of Feng Shui is the Tao of the heart.

About The Author

Shan-Tung Hsu, Ph.D., is a renowned Feng Shui consultant who has been practicing and teaching Feng Shui since 1980. Born and raised in Taiwan, he earned his doctorate in fiber chemistry at the University of Washington in Seattle, where he was one of the first T'ai Chi and Ch'i Kung (Qigong) teachers, and also one of the first to hold classes in Feng Shui. He founded the Blue Mountain Feng Shui Institute to promote an accurate understanding of Feng Shui. The main school is in Seattle, Washington, and there is a branch school in San Juan, Puerto Rico. Shan-Tung Hsu has traveled extensively in Asia, Europe and the Americas providing lectures and consultation services. His studies with traditional teachers, beginning with his family tradition, combined with his scientific background, have given him unique qualifications for building bridges between this ancient art and the modern world. He is extensively involved in qi (ch'i) research, is publisher of the World Qigong Magazine, and has served on the Standing Committee of the World Medical Qigong Association. His client list includes large corporations and architectural, construction, and landscape design firms, as well as private individuals.